THE
WILSON
READING
SYSTEM

STUDENT
READER
SEVEN

by Barbara A. Wilson

SECOND EDITION

Wilson Language Training
162 West Main Street
Millbury, Massachusetts 01527-1943
(508) 865-5699

The Reading Program
(408) 262-1349

ISBN 1-56778-018-0 8.00 Student Reader Seven   Item# SR7

ISBN 1-56778-011-3 33.00 Student Readers 7-12   Item# WRS712

ISBN 1-56778-009-1 78.00 Student Readers 1-12   Item# WRS112

ISBN 1-56778-000-8 196.00 WRS Complete Set   Item# WRS101

The Wilson Reading System is published by:

Wilson Language Training
162 West Main Street
Millbury, MA 01527-1943

Printed in the U.S.A.

S T E P

7

Concepts

7.1   - Sound options: c {e, i, y} (concentrate, concede)
               g {e, i, y} (gentle, pungent)

7.2   - ge, ce, dge (lunge, indulgence, pudge)

7.3   - New digraphs: ck, ph, tch (hemlock, pamphlet, fetch)

7.4   - tion, sion (subtraction, expansion)

pace	stage	rice
truce	wage	cent
rage	place	price
cinch	twice	huge
face	gene	spruce

---

spice	cite	page
lace	loge	cell
gem	space	ice
age	lice	brace
ace	nice	cage

---

tangent	process	vigil
decent	tragic	embrace
giblet	citrus	enrage
decide	legend	civil
agent	citric	gentry

---

cyclone	except	giant
civics	rampage	princess
cogent	pencil	recent
placid	abscess	pungent
disgrace	precede	sincere

---

recess	congest	cypress
stingy	cyclops	fancy
recede	advice	angel
cycle	ingest	city
gyro	Nancy	accept

---

success	stencil	digest
priceless	dingy	cancel
oblige	transcend	concept
access	census	suggest
cecede	engage	accent

civilize	gelatin	decency
genetic	incident	regency
cyanide	gentleman	anticipate
contingent	innocent	fugitive
citizen	gigantic	homicide

---

geologist	emancipate	longitude
potency	astringent	reciprocate
indulgent	deficit	gyrostat
contingency	diligent	infancy
centipede	engagement	accident

---

concede	excite	coma
gala	refuge	hiccup
replace	Cindy	spicy
crescent	golden	rancid
magic	cobra	ascend

thrice	gobble	racist
guzzle	legend	centrum
coincide	spacecraft	adjacent
cult	Celtics	gambrel
agency	concentrate	gentle

gelt	blace	gint
cilt	cest	boce
prace	struge	gilb
glest	clem	ploge
geft	cide	gump

---

clim	ceff	grote
cimp	ging	crin
gede	gend	cipe
cere	cive	frage
gind	fice	bloge

---

plogy	comlige	cynet
flegent	occint	glomece
crintage	trinpoce	filcy
celtone	decepe	regist
centope	trimcel	tringy

---

plevice	dilgene	gintly
trincy	ginmope	brency
regage	gytrone	placent
stengil	receme	gymote
inscroge	centrome	gromece

---

1. Nancy did not like to gamble a cent!

2. Steve had to get a brace on his leg after he fell off the cycle.

3. Jim is quite restless to find out the price of the condo in Boston.

4. I think that price will enrage him!

5. Regretfully, I must cancel my next date with Ed so that I can complete this job.

6. Jane was frequently complimented on her nice, fancy dress.

7. Bob suggested that Teddy should play baseball in the spring.

8. Is there space in the old shed for this giant cage?

9. Hopefully, Jim will do the magic for the kids.

10. The boss wished that Tom was finished with the last page.

1. The cops witnessed the incident on Gentome St.

2. Ed thinks that the Celtics will clinch first place again.

3. Tim jumped up and gave his mom a huge embrace.

4. Dad wisely expressed his advice.

5. Mom was quite congested, so she had to go to the clinic.

6. The delinquents went on a rampage and demolished the stage set.

7. Dad insisted that he would make the giblet gravy.

8. The tragic accident happened because of carelessness.

9. We will get a small refund when we recycle these cans.

10. Jill requested that her dad tell her the tale of the princess.

1. Our company must keep pace in this competitive city.

2. There is a distinct spice in this cake, but I can't identify it.

3. Bob has a decent job at the Centrum.

4. Mr. Hopkins could be a secret agent.

5. I hope we find a place of refuge – I need to rest!

6. Nancy and Bill are quite stingy and refuse to help the family.

7. Ted has been unable to acquire access to the files.

8. Gram is finished with the dress – lace and all!

9. Recess is a requirement; therefore, you must give the students a break.

10. The democratic process is quite complex.

7.1

1. Jake sincerely hopes that Wendy will go on a date with him.

2. The engagement of Steve and Sally was quite unexpected!

3. I must request complete quiet so that I can concentrate to finish this task.

4. Benny was found innocent of all crimes.

5. I think the potency of these pills made me quite dizzy.

6. I will be indulgent after the basketball game and go get ice cream.

7. Beth's date, Sam, was quite a gentleman!

8. The kids could not decide, so Mr. Billings suggested a democratic vote.

9. James is a U.S. citizen, but his wife is a citizen of Finland.

10. Tammy witnessed the escape of a fugitive.

Fugitive Rampage

The F.B.I. was called to investigate. The agent came to the scene* to find expensive gems stolen from a home in the city of Los Angeles. Despite extensive planning, a trespasser had been able to get entry.

Recently, there were many such crimes in fine L.A. homes. The F.B.I. suspected a fugitive who had gone on a similar rampage in Cincinatti. One innocent citizen had been killed already. The F.B.I. wanted to prevent any more tragic incidents.

* *scene* - The s and c together say /s/. *Scent* and *science* are other examples

Nancy's Braces

Nancy's dentist suggested that she should get braces. Nancy did not expect this advice, but he sincerely felt it would be an effective way to prevent problems. He would have to extract a tooth to make more space.

Nancy asked about the price of the braces. It was a disgrace! They were quite expensive. She felt like she was too old as well. She was twenty-six and had recently begun a sales job. She did not want braces to upset her smile.

Nancy had to decide. Most of the cost would be refundable. She could not let her age prevent her if it would be best in the long-run. She restlessly mulled it over. Her husband successfully convinced her that it would not be bad. The dentist told her that she would not regret it. At last, Nancy set the date to have it done.

Magic

At recess time, a man came to Centrum High School to do magic. Mike said that he could figure it out. He felt it would be a cinch. Dave said, "O.K. then, let's wage a small bet." Mike accepted.

The man on stage began his magic. He had a princess doll in a cage. He chanted a tune and held a cloth over the cage. When he lifted it, the cage was gone and he held a giant pencil. It was impossible to guess!*. The man did the trick twice. Mike did concentrate, but he could not figure it out. Silently, Dave held out his hand to collect the cash from the bet.

* *guess* - The <u>u</u> acts to maintain the hard sound of g. It is silent. Other words with u as a 'buffer': *guest, guild, guilt, Guiness.*

Space Age Skit

The Belmont High School freshmen class was planning a skit for Class Day. Jenny was a ham, but Cathy did not wish to be in the skit. Jenny said to her friend, "No problem! It will be a cinch. You will love it on stage!"

The skit was about the Space Age. Twice, Cathy wanted to quit, but Jenny insisted that she do it. On the day of the skit, Cathy's hands felt like ice. She did not want to face the crowd.

The Space Age skit was the last to go on stage. Cathy did it! She was so glad to finish, and it was a huge success.

lunge	trance	tinge
confidence	flange	wince
hinge	evidence	diligence
sixpence	plunge	advance
infringe	fragrance	expunge

---

entrance	fringe	lance
cadence	convince	singe
distance	challenge	fence
scrunge	existence	impinge
insistence	indulgence	extravagance

7.2

smudge	sledge	dodge
badge	drudge	trudge
fledge	lodge	dredge
grudge	edge	Madge
wedge	fudge	bridge

---

dge, nce, nge

budge	dredge	ridge
ledge	nudge	judge
sludge	since	pudge
intelligence	twinge	grudge
Rutledge	hodgepodge	condolence

---

1. Suddenly, the cop had to lunge at the gunman in the bank hold-up.

2. Jim drove until he could find the entrance to the mall.

3. Kate has lots of confidence, but her date, Tom, is quite shy.

4. I plan on witnessing the big event when Bob and Tim plunge into the icy, cold pond.

5. The detective must find more evidence for his most recent case.

6. I want to indulge in a fattening, vanilla ice cream cone!

7. Dad has to help Hank construct a fence.

8. At his wife's insistence, Ted went to the job agency for help.

9. Henry asked Betsy for advice on which kind of fragrance to buy for Kate.

10. Ron was thankful when his boss gave him a big cash advance.

1. The existence of the will helped solve all the family disputes.

2. Bill's incredible intelligence is sometimes hidden by his shyness.

3. A square dance will be held at the lodge on July 10th.

4. Mr. Prince requested complete silence, but the class did not stop talking.

5. This publishing project has instilled Ed with lots of confidence.

6. You need a press badge to get into the big event.

7. Tammy sat at the edge of her bed to contemplate what to do.

8. There will be a hodgepodge of items for sale to make money for softball.

9. The kids like to play dodge ball at recess.

10. Betsy did not want to smudge her make-up, so she would not jump in the lake.

1. Since the race, Tom has not run any distance at all.

2. I like the fringe on the sides of that dress.

3. Madge had a bridge game at the club.

4. If you win the bet it will entitle you to a huge piece of fudge.

5. Carefully, James inched along the rocky ledge.

6. The judge must sentence the juvenile delinquent.

7. It is regretful that Mr. Plonce holds such a grudge against his dad.

8. The requirements of the class present a huge challenge to the students.

9. Jane helped me convince Sandra to go on the fast amusement ride.

10. Mom will not budge from her position that the investment will be too costly.

The Elk's Lodge

The Elk's lodge had become a bit run-down. Randy suggested that each member contribute to fix the place. If they accepted the challenge, then Randy had confidence that the job could be completed by June. He did not anticipate any problems since the job was small.

Randy gave evidence that the lodge needed repair. The entrance hall was dingy, the fence along the drive was broken and the shingles needed paint. At his insistence, the Elks finally did decide to make the repairs. The lodge did not need to be fancy, but it would be nice to spruce up the place.

Indulgence

Madge loved extravagance! Since she and Steve invested in the condo, she wished to get expensive items to fill it. Steve told her that they could not afford such indulgences, but he did not convince her.

Madge was able to get many things and still stay within the budget. She felt it was a thrilling challenge. Madge told Steve about each new item in advance. This was because of his insistence. Most of the time Steve was fond of the prospective purchase as well.

In time, Steve could see that Madge was entirely respectful of the budget. This did silence his protests, and Madge had fun as she expressively filled her home.

sphere	graph	dolphin
humph	Joseph	emphasis
cellophane	phonograph	telephone
prophet	stratosphere	monograph
geography	alphabet	Philip

---

phone	atmosphere	phantom
sphinx	graphite	triumph
photo	phase	hyphen
Ralph	phrase	photograph
phosphide	graphic	pamphlet

---

batch	notch	itch
stitch	splotch	Dutch
flitch	etch	patch
latch	ditch	stretch
crotch	hatch	crutch

---

match	glitch	thatch
switch	ratch	hutch
pitch	scotch	catch
blotch	ketch	twitch
snatch	botch	fetch

---

crutches	ratchet	kitchen
dispatch	Gretchen	satchel
ketchup	Mitchell	hatchet
switch	Scotch	pitch
hitch	scratch	witch

---

ck

quack	fleck	track
mock	speck	neck
smock	muck	pock
lack	crock	lick
duck	back	puck

Dick	deck	nick
clock	trick	stuck
kick	sock	luck
flick	cluck	flock
stack	rock	struck

---

click	frock	chick
rack	shuck	smack
pluck	click	lack
stock	hack	stick
mock	pick	Huck

---

chicken	bucket	jacket
lipstick	rocket	haddock
attack	wicket	hemlock
pocket	stricken	flintlock
ransack	cricket	shamrock

---

crackle	buckle	fickle
chuckle	freckle	trickle
tackle	cockle	sickle
tickle	spackle	pickle
cackle	shackle	suckle

---

1. Joseph suggested that we go see his prospective land investment.

2. The kids wanted to go see the dolphins again.

3. Lately, Bob has been rude; I hope it is just a phase!

4. When the Celtics triumph, the fans in Boston go wild!

5. Philip had to ask his dad for advice about his old Dodge van.

6. The phone call established a contact with the big company.

7. James was quite upset when he lost the photograph of Wendy.

8. I must get cellophane next time I shop.

9. Mom was grateful when Dad helped Sandy with the alphabet.

10. We will send you a pamphlet to describe the retirement plan.

7.3

1. Did the Dutch and English settle in that colony?

2. Tim had a big scratch on his leg from the tomcat.

3. Sam drenched his hotdog in ketchup!

4. Since Randy could not catch the ball, the dog had to fetch it.

5. Sandra was still on crutches from her accident last June.

6. Helpfully, Gram will stitch up this dress for the banquet.

7. Did Ted find the hatchet in the old shed?

8. I will not go to the dance because I am so itchy from the sun.

9. Bev gave Pam a kitchen witch that matched her red drapes.

10. Ralph just wanted to stretch out on the cot, but he had to make lunch.

1. Dick did not fumble the ball, but he still did not play well.

2. The clock was demolished when it struck the table.

3. The kids sat in amazement as Tom did his magic tricks.

4. Ed had no difficulty finishing the big stack of pancakes.

5. Kim had to freshen up after she ran around the track ten times.

6. We must hang this shamrock for St. Patrick's Day.

7. Fred had lipstick on his neck!

8. It will take us a long time to fill this bucket with clams.

9. The cops had the kid empty his pockets on the table.

10. I missed the rocket blast-off when the postponement was prolonged.

1. Ted made the best tackle in the Thanksgiving Day match.

2. Sandy did chuckle when Jim spilled the ketchup on his pants.

3. Ben had a big freckle on his neck.

4. Phil munched on the chicken wings, but Fred did not eat.

5. Ben struck his nose on a rock when he fell in the ditch.

6. Pam was so fickle that she could not decide who to date.

7. Ed checked the stock in the kitchen.

8. Fred held the trump ace in the game of pitch, so he felt quite confident.

9. Next, the boss will dispatch the vans to pick up the junk.

10. Betsy was lucky when she got seven pickles on her plate.

Dolphin Land

Ralph gave Joseph a telephone call. Dolphin Land had requested a photograph for a new pamphlet to be given to the travel agency. Ralph asked Joseph to do the job.

Joseph felt it would be fun. He spent the day at Dolphin Land. He was able to get many photographs. The pamphlet was made to emphasize the playfulness of the dolphins. This was not difficult. Hopefully, the pamphlet would get people to visit the eventful place called Dolphin Land.

7.3

tch

outside	chair
turn	hospital
light	sprain
floor	someone
over	else

Gretchen's Visit

Gretchen and Philip Smith went to visit the Mitchells. They sat outside and grilled hotdogs. Gretchen wished to be helpful and went into the kitchen for the bottle of ketchup. She could not find the switch to turn on the light.

All of a sudden, there was a big crash. Philip and the Mitchells ran to the kitchen. Gretchen was on the floor with the hutch on top of her leg! Phil and Tom Mitchell had to hustle over and lift it off her.

Gretchen could only hobble to a chair. Her ankle was red and swelling. She did not want to go to the hospital, but she had to.

At nine o'clock, Gretchen limped back into the Mitchell's kitchen. This time she was on crutches! She was quite thankful that her ankle was not broken. The accident had resulted in a bad sprain.

"I'm all set for a hot dog," Gretchen said. "But this time, I'll let someone else get the bottle of ketchup!"

Dick Tackles the Stack

Dick had to attack the complex job. He had a stack of documents that he had to tackle before Monday. He intended to finally complete the task.

Dick got a tall glass of lemonade and hid from the T.V. He went out on the deck where he could not be distracted by the ballgame. He had to stick to the job until it was complete.

Dick did not go back inside until five o'clock. He was glad to have a decent plan to submit to his boss. He missed the game, but he finished the difficult task at last.

subtraction	constitution	prescription
reception	introduction	ventilation
instruction	solution	regulation
compensation	execution	fiction
congestion	devotion	prevention

digestion	suggestion	eruption
objection	location	option
intention	reproduction	protection
education	promotion	infection
mention	investigation	dictation

temptation	consumption	sensation
salvation	mutation	probation
digestion	exemption	traction
vocation	emotion	relaxation
domination	consolation	imposition

---

application	reclamation	desolation
elocution	delegation	illustration
exultation	description	quotation
condensation	invention	abduction
conjunction	lotion	conviction

---

fixation	addiction	pollution
excretion	infraction	inflation
ration	suction	indignation
commendation	constellation	locomotion
liquidation	implication	production

---

condition	addition	cognition
contrition	petition	opposition
competition	disposition	expedition
imposition	definition	nutrition
ignition	volition	munition

---

ramification stabilization civilization

specification notification utilization

modification minimization codification

edification pacification unification

ratification notification gratification

---

colonization capitalization intensification

regimentation manifestation exemplification

hospitalization rehabilitation monopolization

representation solidification excommunication

electrification humanization recommendation

---

mansion   pension   tension

impulsion   compulsion   expansion

suspension   extension   convulsion

dissension   ascension   pretension

repulsion   revulsion   expulsion

---

propulsion   dimension   declension

reprehension   comprehension   recension

apprehension   condescension   expansionist

pensioned   emersion   dispersion

immersion   declension   dimensionless

---

passion	mission	session
fission	cession	confession
admission	discussion	regression
depression	progression	repression
digression	commission	concession

---

aggression	impression	impassion
submission	expression	remission
recession	omission	profession
succession	concussion	compassion
obsession	possession	oppression

7.4

vision	fusion	lesion
abrasion	intrusion	exclusion
invasion	collision	transfusion
occasion	confusion	conclusion
explosion	adhesion	obtrusion

---

diffusion	allusion	incision
decision	division	implosion
collusion	television	illusion
precision	evasion	provision
protrusion	cohesion	revision

---

conjunction	satisfaction	occasion
confession	civilization	indication
collision	discussion	registration
calculation	explosion	institution
invasion	admission	dimension

---

precision	cultivation	concussion
combination	isolation	exclusion
compassion	education	definition
introduction	protrusion	suspension
depression	notification	indication

---

1. The Smiths will be able to host a reception for Mr. Cosby.

2. With just a little instruction, I was able to win at tennis.

3. The salesman handed out pamphlets as an introduction to his product.

4. Relocation is the only solution to our company's space problem.

5. Bill made the suggestion that we travel to the lake for some relaxation.

6. The detective must conduct an intensive investigation into that difficult case.

7. The plan must present some options so that the boss can make a selection.

8. Danny was given a big promotion when he had a successful trip to China.

9. Ben had to complete the job application and then hope for the best.

10. Jim and Peg felt the temptation to travel to Africa.

1. Tom helped with the music production for that rock band.

2. It was difficult to get a description of the useful invention.

3. Steve's drug addiction is so sad.

4. That company will have a liquidation sale, and I think we will be able to find a desk.

5. I think the pollution in this city is disgusting!

6. The witness will hopefully give a consistent description of the delinquent.

7. When I complete the addition, will you do the subtraction?

8. The Wisconsin clinic intends to present topics on nutrition in the month of July.

9. If we go to Atlantic City, there will be little time for relaxation.

10. He gave Jim the recommendation to establish an alcohol rehabilitation program.

7.4

1. Madge willingly went to the bridge game held at the gentleman's mansion.

2. Joseph will get a decent pension after his retirement.

3. Jane innocently asked a question that left tension in the club.

4. The kids in Mrs. Billing's class will use the reading comprehension books.

5. Bob had to take exact dimensions to make a kitchen cabinet for his wife.

6. The company is planning a big expansion in late spring.

7. Joseph had to ask his boss for an extension on the publishing project.

8. Jane and Bob have a little apprehension about the sale.

9. Jake was given a suspension for his disrespectful attitude.

10. The loss was because of the bad dissension on the team.

1. Jim completely lost his vision in the bad accident.

2. There was a lot of confusion after the explosion.

3. The men had to carefully plan the invasion into the jungle.

4. Ed willingly helped lift the television onto the van.

5. Edna had to provide the Navy with their provisions.

6. Mr. Jones will have a blood transfusion to prevent another attack.

7. The conclusion of the Olympics will be an impressive event.

8. The boss will make his decision about the contract this month.

9. It will be a big occasion when the princess visits this nation.

10. Jake will get a big fine for tax evasion.

7.4

1. Dad has compassion for those made helpless by the tragic quake in Mexico.

2. Jane wished that she had help with the math calculations.

3. The club engaged in exclusion by establishing a policy which discriminated by race.

4. Bob had to sit in isolation because he disrupted the class.

5. Babs got such satisfaction when her students made excellent progress.

6. Joseph had to find the definition of the word "illusion."

7. The regulations for education in this state are quite complex.

8. Nancy must check the collision policy she has on the van.

9. Jake wanted to give Madge the notification of her new position.

10. I think Ted will get a suspension for cutting class again.

1. Betsy had a bad abrasion on her leg.

2. The delinquent gave his confession to the detective.

3. Regretfully, the discussion did not seem to help Pam's confidence.

4. The king is adept with his delegation of duty.

5. I asked the boss for a concrete definition of my role here.

6. Cathy's new car handles with precision.

7. Jane gave no indication of her plans when she quit her job.

8. Janice must decide if she will accept that position at the bank.

9. When the tickets went on sale at the Centrum, there was a lot of confusion.

10. Jim had no intention of missing class, but his van got a flat tire.

A Position in Judge Phillip's Office

Janice Mitchell filled out an application for a job in the office of Judge Sandra Phillips. The judge was kind, and Janice felt that she would be exciting to work for. Janice had confidence that she could do the job. She had the intention to somehow secure the position.

Janice had to figure out a plan. She knew that a reception was to be held at the city hall. Judge Phillips would be attending it. Janice made plans to go and introduce herself to the judge. She would mention her hope for the office job. Possibly she could convince the judge to hire her for the open position. She felt the excitement of anticipation.

Janice went to the reception with her plan in mind. She did not wish to be an imposition on Judge Phillips, yet she intended to meet her. At last Janice saw the judge standing alone. She went up to her and held out her hand. The judge recognized her face but could not place her. Quickly, Janice told her that she was an applicant for the office position. Sandra Phillips was impressed with Ms. Mitchell's confidence and determination.

The next day, Judge Phillips went to her office. She had many applications to select from. One name stood out – Janice Mitchell. The judge carefully read the application. She was happy.

At last she picked up the phone to make the call to Ms. Mitchell. Janice gladly accepted the job.

Tom and Meg's Bronco

Jim and Tom went for a ride in Tom's Bronco jeep. Since the last trip, it had not run well. Jim suggested that the transmission had a problem. This made Tom upset.

When Tom and Jim got back home, Tom told his wife, Meg. She did not want to replace the transmission. They could not spend much cash to fix the Bronco. They had to hope that it was not a big problem.

Tom went to the gas station with the Bronco to find out about its condition. The place was quite busy, and the man could not check it out until after lunch.

At last, a diagnosis was made. It was not the transmission! It would be a cinch to fix. Tom and Meg were quite glad. The price of the job was not very much. Soon the Bronco was in fine shape again.

The Price of Progress

Teddy's boss, Mr. Lance, called him into his office. He wanted to send Teddy on a mission to find out about their competition. A copy and print shop was opening across the street!

Teddy went to the new shop. It was not open yet, but the door was unlocked. Teddy made the decision to go in. He gave the impression that he wanted a printing job done.

The shop was quite impressive! It had twice the equipment as Mr. Lance's little shop. Teddy left it feeling quite sad. He did not want to tell his boss.

When Teddy went back to his shop, he could see the apprehension on Mr. Lance's face. Teddy's expression said it all. He did not even tell his boss about the new place. Mr. Lance just went into his office and quietly shut the door.

friend
usually
see
movie
watch
door
tomorrow
night

Decision to Shop

Jane got a call from her friend, Betty. Betty wanted to go shopping at the mall. Usually, Jane would go, but she was just getting set to see the conclusion of a movie called <u>The Last Invasion from Space</u>. Jane made the decision to see the final segment since she had spent the evening before watching the beginning.

Jane asked Betty if she wanted to visit and see the movie. Betty did not like television but she occasionally watched it. She did not wish to see <u>The Last Invasion from Space</u>, but she felt it would be nice to see Jane.

Betty drove across the city to Jane's apartment. Jane had her jacket on and met Betty at the door. "There is a revision in the plan," said Jane. "We can shop after all. There is some confusion with programming, so the movie's conclusion will be on tomorrow night."

Post Test Step Seven

pungent	diligence	hyphen
sledge	ketch	progression
ransack	consumption	adjacent
infection	cyclops	trudge
gyrostat	expunge	intrusion

---

ronvince	tricken	rovision
fincantation	phosphile	litch
nivision	demission	bation
tringy	ginmope	boce
cimp	comlige	stimgage
